595 Green

AF574162

# Stagbeetles

Adapted by Anthony Wootton
from an idea by Toyoaki Ozaki
Illustrated by Kazuhiro Yoshioka

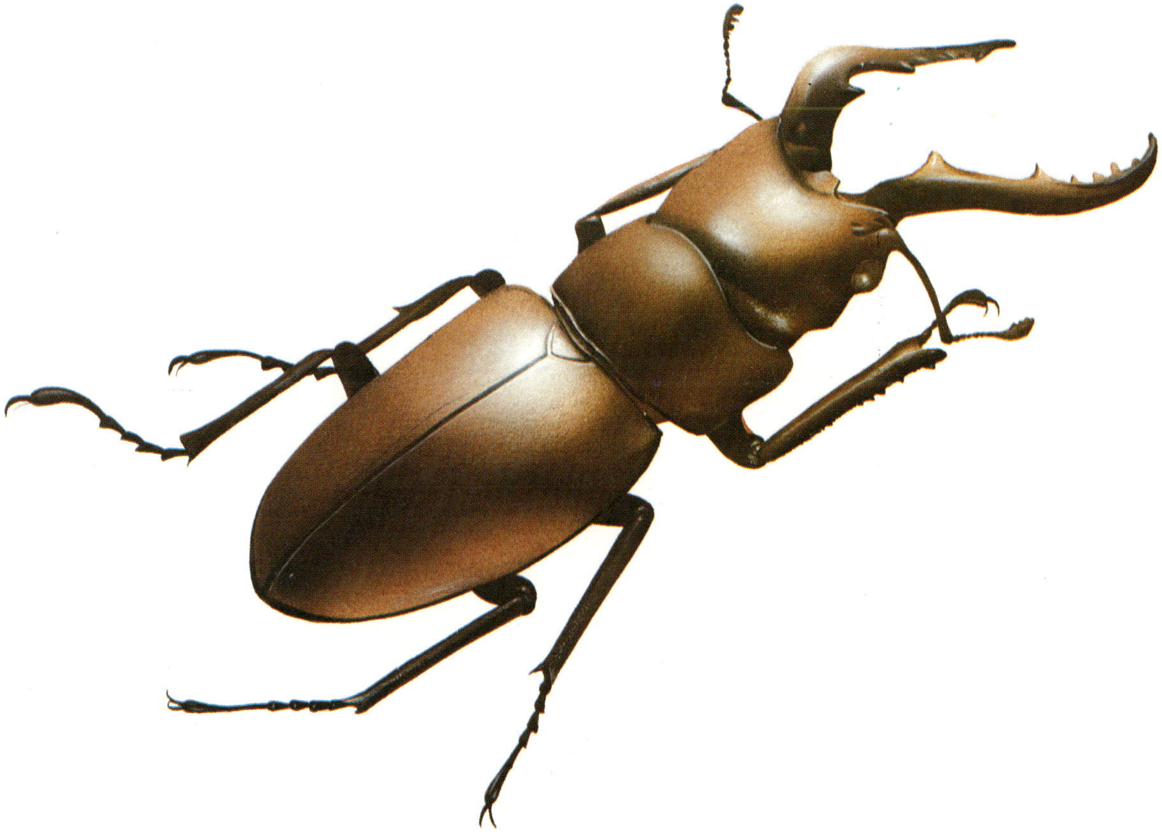

Wayland

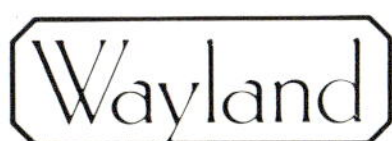

These are the 'antlers' of a stagbeetle. They look like the horns of a stag, or a male deer, don't they?

Their antlers are not really horns, of course. They are large jaws. Only the male stagbeetle has jaws shaped like this. Here is the stagbeetle itself – a male. Stagbeetles are mostly found in woods, because their young feed on the rotting stumps of old trees.

Male stagbeetles use their horns to frighten their enemies and to challenge other male stagbeetles. They even use them to attract females!

Male stagbeetles don't use their huge jaws to capture food. They can only take liquids. This stagbeetle is sucking up the sweet sap of a tree, using its special tongue. Sometimes it uses its horns to pierce the skin of fruit, and then suck up the juice.

There are many kinds of stagbeetles in different parts of the world. There are about nine hundred known kinds. Here are just a few of them. All these come from the Far East and Japan.

If you turn a stagbeetle over, you can see how its body works. The beetle's body is separated into three parts: head, thorax and abdomen. The jaws, mouth, eyes, and antennae (or feelers) are on the head. The antennae are used to smell food or to recognize other insects.

The stagbeetle has one pair of wings and three pairs of legs. These are attached to the thorax.

The abdomen contains the beetle's heart and digestive and sexual parts.

If you look at the beetle's legs, you will see they have little claws at the tips which help it to cling to tree trunks.

The male stagbeetle's head is much larger than the female's, to carry his enormous jaws. But the female's jaws are sharper and stronger than the male's.

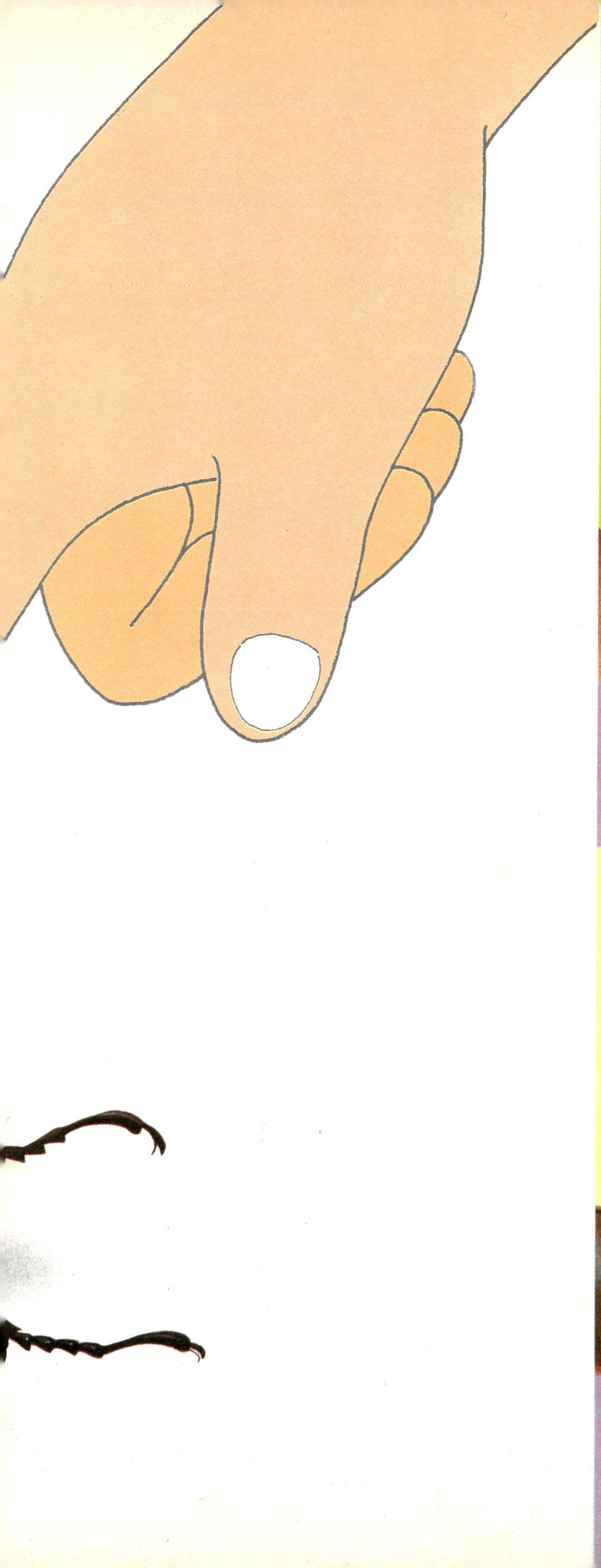

If you point a finger at a stagbeetle it may spread its jaws threateningly. The male's jaws are harmless and can only give a little pinch.

But the female's jaws are sharp and powerful. She uses them to dig out holes in rotting tree stumps, in which she lays her eggs.

If you touch a stagbeetle on its head or thorax, it may rear up angrily. It often falls over on its back and then it cannot turn over again, because its jaws and body are very heavy.

Stagbeetles like sweet things. Here a male and female are drinking the juice from an apple. Sometimes they drink drops of beer spilt in the gardens of pubs!

Perhaps you did not know that a stagbeetle can fly! It can fly very well. Its wings are protected by wing-covers attached to its abdomen. When stagbeetles fly, the wing-covers are held up high and wide so as not to get in the way of the wings. They often fly on warm summer evenings and sometimes fly indoors around electric lamps.

Lots of other insects can fly, too, of course. Here is a dragonfly which has turned a somersault before keeping on the same line of flight.

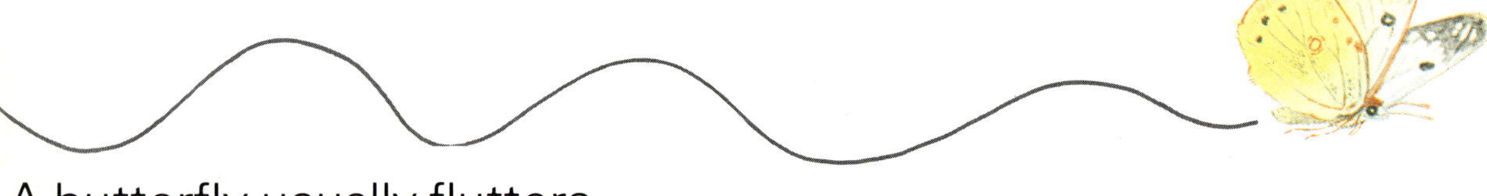

A butterfly usually flutters.

The stagbeetle flies noisily and never very far. In midsummer, male and female stagbeetles mate. The male stagbeetle finds his partner on trees, especially oaks. He may circle the tree several times before deciding where to land.

Decaying trees provide food for stagbeetles. Here the female has laid her eggs in a little hole in a rotting tree trunk. She has dug out the holes with her jaws and with her powerful forelegs.

The young beetles (larvae) hatch from the eggs and feed on the decaying wood which they burrow into. Later the larva turns into a chrysalis and then the chrysalis turns into the adult beetle. The beetle finally pushes its way out of the wood.

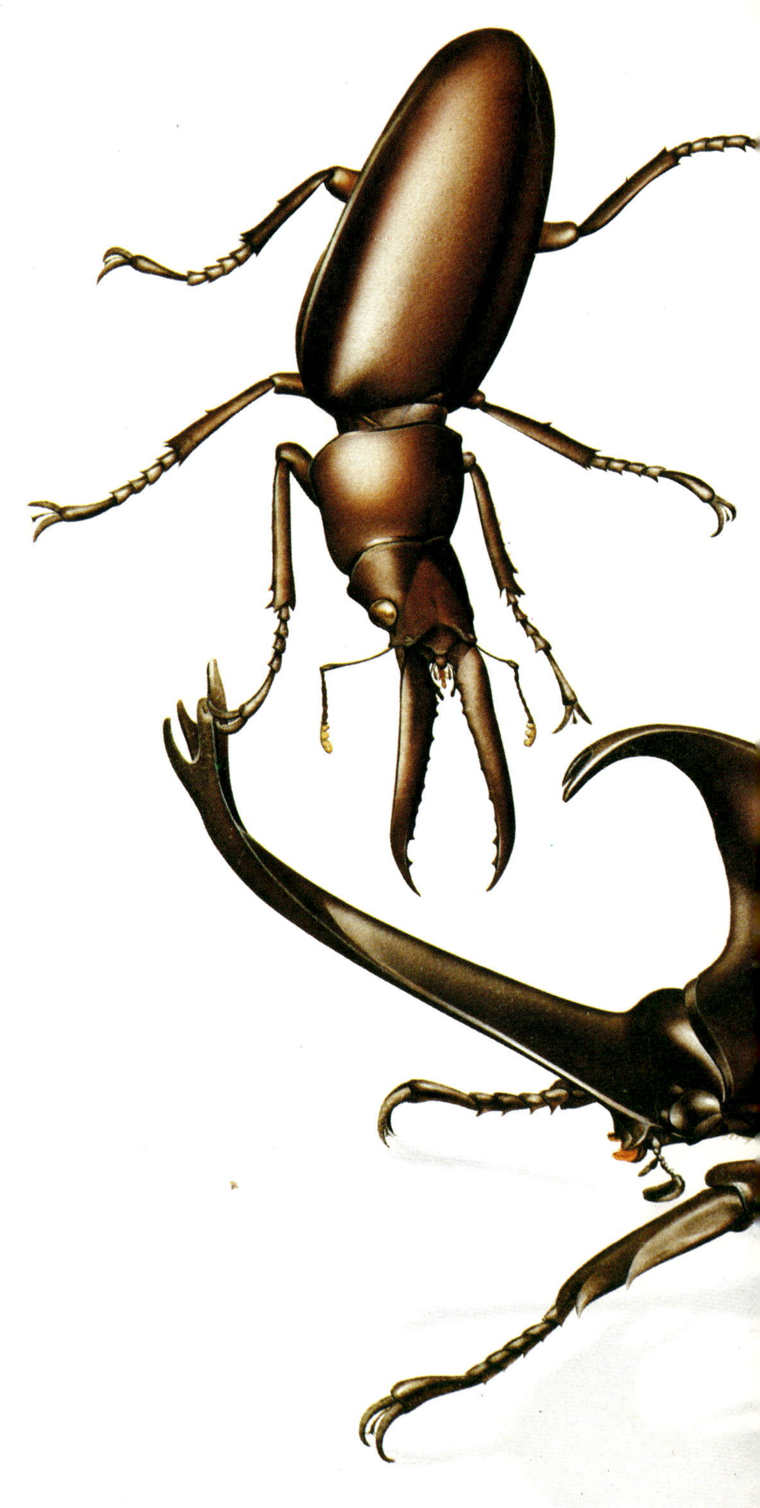

There are many other kinds of beetles with strangely shaped jaws. One kind is called the Rhinoceros beetle. You can see its long spiked jaw which is branched at the tip. The stag and the rhinoceros beetles have six legs, wings and wing-covers, and hard bodies. The rhinoceros beetle is much heavier and thicker than the stagbeetle. Some rhinoceros beetles are among the biggest and heaviest insects in the world.

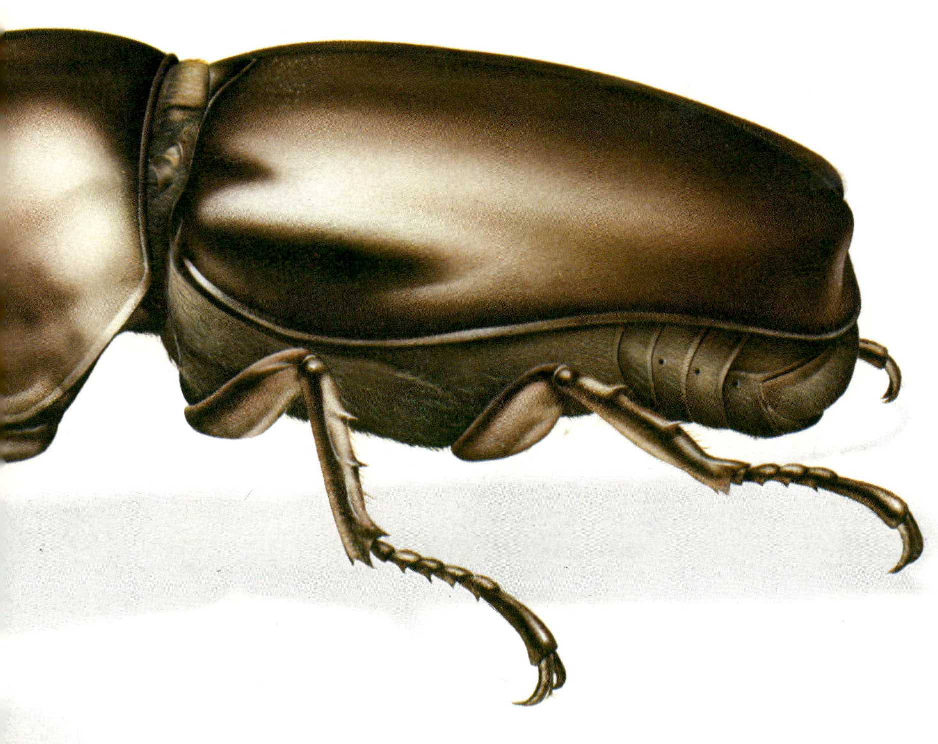

## More about stagbeetles

There are about nine hundred different kinds of stagbeetle to be found in various parts of the world. They vary a lot in size, and in the shape of their jaws. You will have to go abroad, especially to tropical countries, to see some of the more spectacular ones, although some may be seen in museums.

In Britain there are only three species of stagbeetle. The biggest of them is like the one shown in this book. It is found in woods, mainly in southern England, particularly in places like the New Forest in Hampshire. Another kind, the Lesser Stagbeetle, is also found in southern England. It doesn't have such large jaws and is smaller and darker in colour than the big stagbeetle. The third, smallest kind, is only about 10–15 mm long. It is often found in old tree stumps. The male has a tiny upturned horn like that of a rhinoceros on its head, and another on its thorax. The female's horns are very much smaller.

All of these species – especially the big stagbeetle – are getting more and more rare today as woods are cut down and the rotting tree stumps in which the larvae feed are cleared away. In some countries the big stagbeetle is now legally protected. Unfortunately this is not so in Britain.

## More about beetles

Stagbeetles are only one kind of beetle. There are a great many more. In fact there are at least two hundred and fifty thousand kinds. Beetles are found in all sorts of places: plants and trees, fruits, hedges and undergrowth; in water, in the soil, under stones and even in houses.

In Britain there are about seven thousand different types, ranging in size from the stagbeetle and the almost equally large Great Silver Water beetle (some 5 cm long) to tiny beetles only a few millimetres long. Some beetles are so small that they are very difficult to find.

Many beetles are of great value to humans. Ladybirds feed on aphids (greenfly and blackfly), and Burying Beetles eat the bodies of dead animals and birds.

Others can be a nuisance – like the Death-Watch Beetle, which causes great damage by gnawing its way through the wooden beams of old buildings.

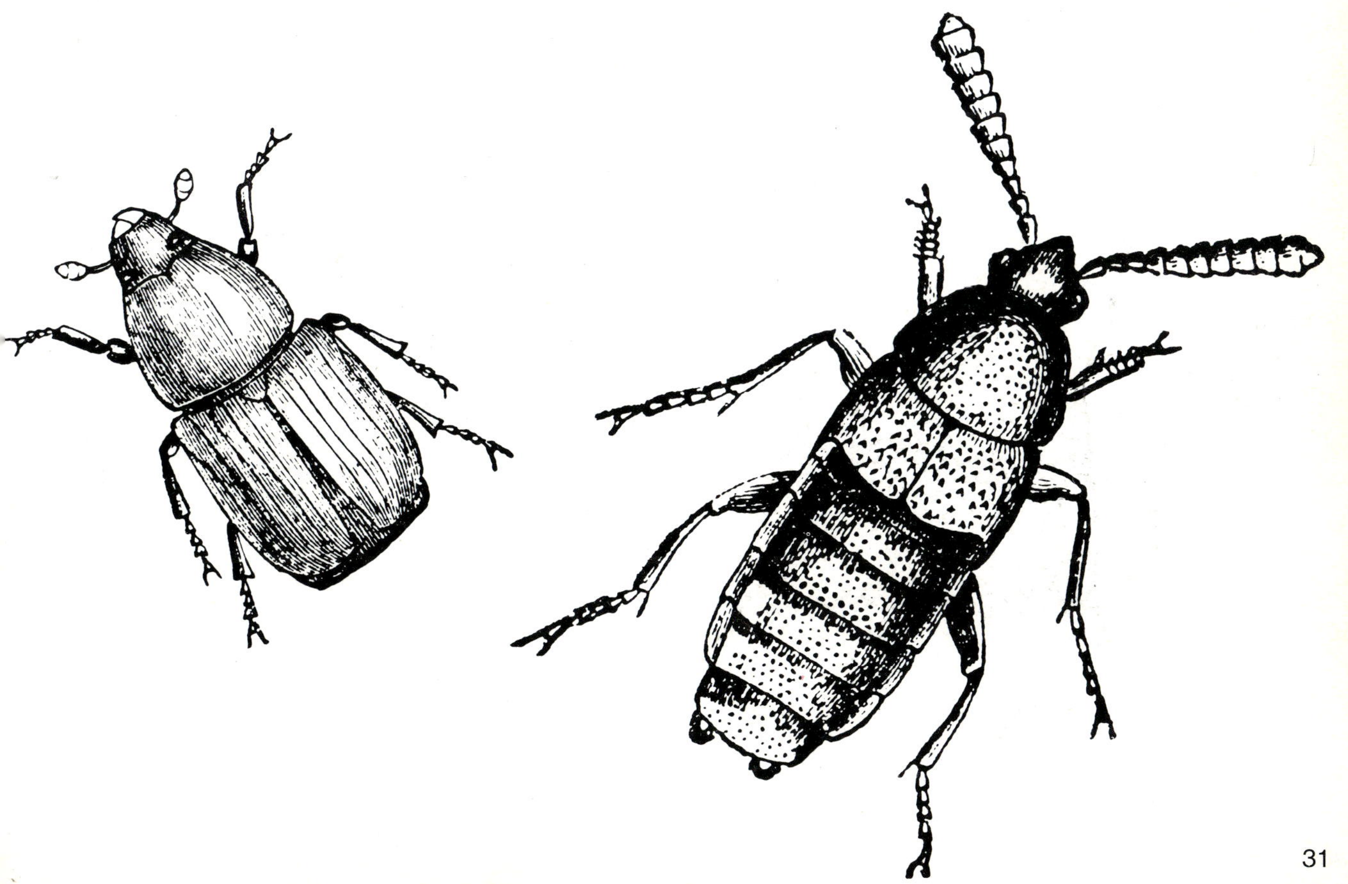

ISBN 0 85340 786 X

Copyright © 1976 by Froebel-Kan Ltd., Tokyo
First published in England in 1980 by
Wayland Publishers Limited
49 Lansdowne Place, Hove
East Sussex BN3 1HF, England
Typeset by Granada Typesetting
Printed in Italy